101 TIPS for Directors

Staff and Parent Self-Esteem

Written by Silvana Clark Illustrated by Priscilla Burris

Warren Publishing House
A Division of Frank Schaffer Publications
Torrance, California

Managing Editor: Kathleen Cubley
Editor: Gayle Bittinger
Contributing Editors: Kate Ffolliott, Susan Hodges, Jean Warren
Copy Editor: Mae Rhodes
Proofreader: Kris Fulsaas
Book Design/Layout: Sarah Ness, Carol DeBolt
Cover Design: Brenda Mann Harrison
Production Manager: Jo Anna Brock

ISBN: 1-57029-075-X

Printed in the United States of America
Published by: Warren Publishing House

Editorial Office: P.O. Box 2250
Everett, WA 98203

Business Office: 23740 Hawthorne Blvd.
Torrance, CA 90505

20 19 18 17 16 15 14 13 12 11 10 9 8 7 6 5 4 3 2

Contents

Making Time for Staff Problems... 4
Staff Incentives and Rewards 6
Parent Self-Esteem 8
Staff Self-Esteem 10
Share the Fun 12
Staff Planning and Involvement.. 14
Reducing Stress for Employees... 16
Ten Ways to Say Thank You 18
Nonverbal Communication......... 20
Staff Problem Solving 22

Making Time for Staff Problems

1 Management by Walk Around (MBWA) is a common business management style often overlooked by early childhood directors. Even though you are busy with administrative duties, take a few minutes at different times of the day to observe employees in action. Observe how they interact with parents in the morning, how they watch children on the playground, and how they serve snacks. This gives you the opportunity to notice problems and assess their negative potential.

2 Provide employees with prompt feedback when their performance doesn't meet your expectations. Waiting and hoping a situation will resolve itself usually won't work. Take the time to remedy staff performance as soon as you notice a problem, before the situation becomes more complex.

3 Explain in a very specific way what you expect of employees. Staff problems occur when you state, "We need to answer the telephone in a professional manner." You may have in mind, "Good morning, this is Mary at the ABC Childcare Center, may I help you?" Teachers may think a professional manner means saying, "Hello, this is Mary." Employees can't meet your standards unless they fully understand what you expect.

4 Prevent potential problems by occasionally asking employees questions such as "What is one thing you would change about the schedule?" "How could we improve the lunch program?" You'll gain valuable insight into how employees view their jobs and how your program is really working.

5 Spend more time listening than you do talking. The best communicators are known for being good listeners. By allowing employees to express their opinions without interruption, you create an atmosphere of caring and trust.

6 Create a working environment where employees feel they can disagree with your opinions. Word spreads quickly when an employer snubs or reprimands someone with a different idea.

7 Management companies frequently use short meetings to handle complaints in a timely fashion. Set a 15- to 20-minute time limit for a meeting and have everyone remain standing. Discuss the situation and attempt to find a solution within the allotted time.

8 Avoid miscommunication problems from the outset by making sure employees understand what you mean. After giving them information or directions, ask them to restate what they think you said. This will clarify your directions before any action takes place.

9 As a director or supervisor, be direct. Make action statements and follow through. Indecisiveness is conveyed when you say, "I'll try to get more paint by tomorrow." Teachers feel frustrated if you don't carry through. Instead, say, "I'll have more paint on Thursday." And then have it there.

10 Employee satisfaction increases when employees are kept informed about work-related issues. Rumors of pay cuts, reduced hours, or changes in staff cause employees to feel uncomfortable. As much as possible, keep employees informed before the rumors begin.

Staff Incentives and Rewards

1 A 1994 Gallup Poll showed the number one cause of employee dissatisfaction was lack of appreciation. When you can't offer high salaries, stock options, or company cars, try other ways of showing employees that you appreciate their contribution to your center.

2 Creativity plays a big part in demonstrating appreciation. Many centers sponsor an "employee of the week" and offer a certificate or small gift. Take that concept one step further and do something like rolling up your sleeves and washing the car of the employee of the week.

3 Certificates, balloons, and even T-shirts play a role in providing staff incentives. Even more important are opportunities for employees to grow professionally. Provide personal feedback to employees, not only at a formal yearly job performance review, but also on an informal weekly or monthly basis.

4 Tailor incentives and rewards to individual employees. A staff member who is a single parent might appreciate a gift certificate for an afternoon of babysitting or a week at summer camp for his or her child. Another employee might be happy to receive a massage or a manicure as an incentive for an attendance goal.

5 If your center is managed by a board of directors or a larger corporation, inform the CEO or board president about outstanding employees. Ask him or her to write letters of appreciation to hardworking staff.

6 Most centers are unable to offer elaborate retirement programs or stock options, but they can provide financial planning information by sponsoring speakers or by distributing brochures. Investment companies will set up a savings program for a nominal monthly commitment.

7 Great care is taken to ensure a clean, safe environment for your children, but what about your employees' environment? Staff need a quiet area with comfortable furniture where they can prepare lesson plans and simply relax. Even a small area designed for their comfort helps employees feel appreciated.

8 Employees also appreciate ways to reduce meal preparation at home. One center made arrangements with a pizza company for employees to order takeout pizzas on Friday night. The pizza company delivered them to the center for easy payment and pickup by staff.

9 Ask employees what motivates them. High salaries are usually not the first priority. Some employees would like flextime, others more creativity in program planning. If possible, reward employees with what they suggest.

10 Interesting work is important to employees. How can you make work more interesting for your staff? Could they have a new schedule? New equipment? Would books or training resources give them a different perspective?

Parent Self-Esteem

1 Call parents at home to share something upbeat about their child. Imagine how a child's parents would respond—after spending a long day at work—to a call from you telling how their son or daughter helped a shy child at school. Your call reinforces parents' confidence in their parenting skills.

2 If you are delayed in fulfilling a promise to parents, simply apologize and tell them what you plan to do. Avoid saying, "I've been really busy," since that suggests they were given low priority on your list of things to do.

3 Children who are in daycare for an extended time often have difficulty reconnecting with their parents at the end of the day. Provide parents with a list of simple ideas to ease the transition time. Ideas could include sharing a snack together on the drive home, reading a short story before leaving the center, or playing together on the playground for a few minutes.

4 If you discover that a parent has been promoted, has given an important speech, or has received a community award, let other parents and staff know. A banner or a sign recognizing the parent's achievement creates a feeling of mutual support and recognition.

5 Provide high-quality name tags for parent volunteers. Professionally made name tags show that you value the person and consider him or her a long-term part of your program.

6 Try not to overburden parents with requests for field trip drivers, cookie bakers, and volunteer coordinators. Many parents want to be involved, but feel guilty if their jobs don't allow them to be active at your center. Let them know they can help according to their time schedules and abilities.

7 Occasionally, ask parents what their needs are, either in person or with a short questionnaire. Try to meet some of those needs. One center that had a lot of families moving in and out of its area found that providing a list of doctors who were accepting new patients really helped overburdened parents. Parents feel included when their needs are also recognized and addressed.

8 If a child used a positive way to handle a conflict or made an extra effort to learn a new skill, let his or her parents know. If you don't have a chance to tell the parents personally, write a short message on a sticky note: "Steven volunteered to sit by a new student today. Ask his teacher to tell you the details." Attach the note to the child's cubby where the parents will see it.

9 Plan a surprise "Parents Are Great" day. Children can help make banners, signs, and cards for their parents. One center had a large cake made with the message *Parents Are Great* on it and served the cake with coffee and milk as parents picked up their children in the afternoon.

10 Parents are always concerned about whether they made the right decision to send their child to your center. Send them a reassuring note thanking them for choosing your program and describing how well their child is adapting to his or her new class.

Staff Self-Esteem

1 General praise is easy to give, but it provides little feedback. Specific praise requires thought and means more to the recipient. Instead of telling an employee, "Thanks for helping with the open house," try a statement such as, "Thank you for the extra effort you made putting up decorations for the open house."

2 "Psychological paychecks" help employees feel their work is noticed. Occasionally, attach a small note to each employee's paycheck with a positive message about his or her efforts at work.

3 Most local newspapers offer a short section highlighting people who have been hired or promoted to a new position. The teacher hired at your center is just as important as the new bank president. Submit notices about training programs completed or academic degrees received by staff as well.

4 Remind staff about the many ways they make a difference in the lives of young children. If a parent makes a positive comment to you about an employee, don't keep it to yourself. Jot down the comment for your files, and then tell the employee as soon as possible. Some centers establish "good apple" awards and list comments made by parents in a prominent location.

5 When a few staff attend a training workshop, ask them to share what they learned with the other employees. Not only does this reinforce learning, it tells staff you value their input.

6 Encourage staff to solve their own problems. If two employees have difficulty getting along, set up a time when they can meet to discuss possible solutions. Intervene as a neutral third party only if they reach a gridlock. Employees feel a greater sense of power when they find a way to overcome a difficulty on their own.

7 Help staff develop additional job skills. If trips to child development conferences are beyond your budget, find other ways to train staff. Provide books, arrange for guest speakers, clip pertinent news articles, and subscribe to professional journals. Employees who feel confident in their job skills develop a greater sense of self-esteem. Ask staff what job skills they would like to develop. An assistant in one preschool said she would like to make up a week's lesson plan. It took more work than she expected, but she felt satisfied with her effort to expand her skills.

8 If it is necessary to reprimand an employee, use factual and specific statements. Phrases such as "You are *always* late" or "You *never* put supplies back in the craft closet" lower a person's self-esteem and don't give a realistic picture of a situation. Instead, make statements like "The records show you've been late to work three times in the past two weeks" or "Eight of our ten watercolor sets are in your room, and Mrs. Nuhn has been looking for them for three days." Stating facts helps you and the employee move on to solutions.

9 Invite staff to participate in an in-house trade show where they set up simple booths or displays showing teaching techniques. Examples of craft projects, new songs, or puppets could be shown. Staff gain recognition for their skills and everyone benefits from new ideas. Parents would also love to see ideas they could adopt for home use. Leave the displays up for the entire day so everyone has a chance to view the exhibit.

10 When an employee makes a suggestion, think about how you usually respond. Do you say, "Let me think about it" and give yourself a chance to look at the possibilities of the idea, or do you respond quickly with, "It would never work; we've tried that before." Make an effort to consider new ideas and eliminate negative phrases from your vocabulary. Also, offer employees the opportunity to try their ideas so they can discover for themselves whether an idea will work or not.

Share the Fun

1 Many companies have established committees designed to provide fun and laughter for employees. Members of the committee decide on ways to bring a bit of joy into the lives of their coworkers. If you have a limited staff, appoint yourself as the official "Fun-Time Expert." One daycare director called herself the "Comical Captain." She began a staff meeting by telling everyone, "Today is Barry Manilow Appreciation Day," and had his tapes playing in the background during the hour-long meeting.

2 Establish a humor bulletin board. Post cartoons, quotes, and short articles. Keep it updated so employees know you place value on joy and laughter at work. Decorate the bulletin board with bright paper and ask for contributions for your "Funny Bones Board." Staff love to bring in silly photos of coworkers.

3 Sponsor fun events that require little time or money but produce positive results. One idea is to take pictures of all employees—from the knees down. Post the photos and have people identify the feet of coworkers. Have vacationing staff members send back crazy postcards. Plan a "tacky tourist" potluck where employees dress in flowered shirts with plaid shorts and bring tacky food to share.

4 Have humorous books, magazines, and tapes available. Any center can have at least one shelf filled with just-for-fun materials to check out. Ask for donations from parents and other employees.

5 Purchase or make buttons and pins to wear. January 21 is National Crazy Hat Day, so have staff come to work with the wildest hat they can find. (You'll find children will want to participate in this event, too.)

6 Bring in a humorous guest speaker for a staff meeting. Local Toastmasters International clubs are delighted to have their members speak for free. Your group gets to hear a new speaker, and the speaker gets experience speaking before an outside audience.

7 Surprise staff and children by decorating the entrance to the center for no special reason. Beginning the day with a walk through streamers and balloons starts everyone on a positive note.

8 Food is a great pick-me-up. Occasionally bring a special snack, other than doughnuts, for employees. How about offering three different varieties of coffee on a Gourmet Coffee Day, or preparing fruit plates with kiwi, orange slices, and strawberries?

9 Periodically give employees "pick-me-up" tips. A few hints on stress reduction or time management printed on a half sheet of paper lets employees know you are thinking about them. Even simple recipes are welcome. Attach the tips to employees' paychecks, mail them to their homes, or even slip the tips under the windshield wipers of their cars.

10 Sharing the fun can also be practical. One director, knowing that employees have little time for car maintenance, arranged for a mobile car repair service to come to the center. The mechanic provided tune-ups for employees' cars without any interruption to their work schedule.

Staff Planning and Involvement

3 Advanced preparation can make in-service training valuable and informative. Distribute a one-page outline on a work-related issue several days ahead of the meeting. At the meeting, give an optional quiz on the material with small prizes for correct answers. This encourages staff to think about the agenda ahead of time.

1 When hiring new employees, have current staff provide input into the selection process. They will be more interested in helping the new person succeed on the job and will be more tolerant of his or her mistakes. Employees might sit in on an interview or critique an activity unit of the applicant's.

2 Involve staff in implementing new ideas as often as possible. Print up "Let's Try This!" cards and keep them in a central location. Employees can fill out a card whenever they have a suggestion. Show staff you value their input by responding to all ideas within 24 hours.

4 Ask staff to take turns being responsible for a portion of a staff meeting. They'll gain valuable leadership skills as well as an awareness of the difficulty involved in handling diverse opinions. They might even appreciate the hard work a director invests in providing quality staff meetings!

5 Encourage staff to try innovative program ideas. Most early childhood centers study themes such as apples or the zoo. Why can't children learn about the Statue of Liberty or even skydiving? By creating an atmosphere where new ideas are encouraged, staff become more creative in their planning.

6 During staff meetings, address employees professionally and with respect. It's easy to say, "You guys have been doing a great job filling out time sheets correctly," but "you guys" brings back memories of junior high school gym class.

7 If major changes need to be made at your center, introduce them to employees gradually. Explain why the changes are taking place and how they will improve working conditions. Ask staff for input on ways they would like to have the changes implemented.

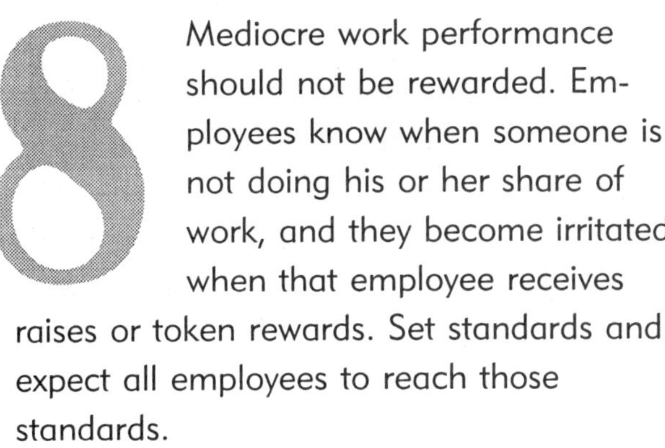

8 Mediocre work performance should not be rewarded. Employees know when someone is not doing his or her share of work, and they become irritated when that employee receives raises or token rewards. Set standards and expect all employees to reach those standards.

9 If you make a mistake, take responsibility for your actions. Making excuses for what happened, such as "It's our policy" or "The board members were pressuring me," undermines your own leadership. Effective leaders admit their mistakes and rectify the situation. Employees respect honest leadership.

10 Leave your office door open unless you are in a confidential meeting. Employees appreciate the symbolic meaning of an open door, even if they don't come in to talk.

Reducing Stress for Employees

1 A key factor in managing stress is to acknowledge the situation in a realistic manner. Ask staff to think about the various situations that cause them stress. As they consider each one, have them ask themselves, "What are the options for handling this situation?" Often a few minutes thinking about realistic solutions will provide one or two workable ideas. Frequently the most realistic solution will be to not worry about it!

2 Encourage staff to develop interests outside their jobs. Post notices of upcoming community concerts or enrichment classes. Occasionally give out gift certificates for a bike rental, an exercise class, or breakfast at a unique restaurant.

3 If you or your staff are facing a difficult situation, try this technique: Imagine how your favorite cartoon character would handle it. Just letting off steam in your head by using some of the character's favorite phrases can reduce the tension and stress of the moment.

4 As an administrator, your disposition and personality can serve as a role model for others. When employees see you handling difficulties with poise and humor, they learn valuable coping skills.

5 When employees are feeling stress about a particular situation, hold a brief brainstorming session with them to generate options. The simple act of recognizing alternatives reduces stress levels.

6 Encourage staff to put their problems in perspective. In the entire scale of life, is it really that serious that your two-year-olds fingerpainted on the carpet when the aide turned her back?

7 Keep a list of quick stress busters in a prominent location. These can include taking several deep breaths, whistling, dancing with the children to lively music, and asking to trade places with a coworker for five minutes. Ask employees to add their favorite ideas to the list.

8 If employees are facing a stressful time, begin a staff meeting by dividing them into small groups. Ask each group to spend three to four minutes writing a song about one of their stress factors. The song should fit the tune of a familiar song. Have the teachers in each group sing their song for the others. This usually produces hearty laughter and also opens discussion about the cause of the stress.

9 To help staff detach from their stress, give each staff member a piece of paper. Ask them to write down the three most stressful things in their lives right now. Have them put their notes in a self-addressed envelope. Collect the envelopes and in three months, mail them to the staff. Often they will discover that what was causing stress earlier is no longer as critical as they thought. This activity also helps staff deal with stress right now by encouraging them to ask, "Three months from now, will this issue still be important to me?"

10 Try innovative ideas to relieve stress. Arrange for a massage therapist to come to the center and give short massages to employees on their break.

Ten Ways to Say Thank You

1 If an employee deserves extra recognition, send a balloon bouquet or flower arrangement to his or her home. The entire family can then participate in the special acknowledgment. Even a simple thank you letter has a bigger impact when sent to the employee's home.

2 When staff need a pick-me-up, plan a "Thank You" day with a garden theme. Have the children decorate the center with tissue paper flowers, ask parents to donate plants, and serve a special lunch with fresh fruit and green salads. Post a big sign saying, "Thank you for helping our children grow!"

3 If an employee deserves a special thank you, find out his or her interests and give a small, related gift. Employees appreciate personal thought behind any gift.

4 Spontaneous time off is an excellent way to thank employees when you want to acknowledge special efforts. Simply go to the teacher and say, "Would you like a 20-minute break? I'll cover your class while you enjoy a cup of coffee." The teacher will appreciate the unexpected few minutes of quiet, and the children will enjoy interacting with you.

5 Say thank you to employees by making staff training fun. Even boring subjects can be energized by trivia contests, work-related games, and appropriate cartoons.

6 Distribute "bright spots" to all employees. These circles, cut out of brightly colored paper, can be used by all employees to acknowledge one another. Encourage employees to write a thank you on a bright spot and give it to a coworker, saying, for example, "Thanks for helping with the rest of my class when Samantha threw up!" Many employees post their bright spots on the wall as a reminder of positive recognition.

7 Thank employees as you pass by in the hall or visit in their classroom. Simple, but effective.

8 Give each employee a red or pink file folder labeled "heart file" to hold positive notes and letters from parents and coworkers. When staff need a psychological boost, they can look in their heart files and be encouraged.

9 Provide humorous personalized achievement awards once in a while. Using calligraphy or a decorative font on a computer, write a specific appreciation statement. For example, "Peter Mills—Outstanding Achievement in Developing 25 Variations on Duck, Duck, Goose." "Allison Collins—Ability to Create Endless Crafts Using Yarn and Fabric Scraps."

10 Chocolate in any form is always appreciated!

Nonverbal Communication

1 A greeting of "Good morning" has little impact when your body language shows you are feeling upset. Parents and staff easily see when nonverbal communication doesn't match your words.

2 Give people your full attention when they talk to you. Direct eye contact is crucial to letting people know you care. Appearing to listen while shuffling papers or glancing at the clock blocks effective communication.

3 Taking notes while a person complains or expresses frustration communicates your concern. The act of listening and jotting down important information shows the other person that you want to get the facts straight. It also helps you to have pertinent information on hand to solve the problem.

4 Hearing and listening are two distinct functions. Anyone can hear cars, horns, and people. Listening requires energy and focused attention. It engages your mind. Allowing employees and parents to talk without interruption is one of the best ways to build self-esteem.

5 Sit or stand up straight as people talk to you. (Naturally, this doesn't apply to the times you need to contort your body to crawl inside a three-year-old's cardboard castle.) Leaning on a wall or slouching in a chair can convey a feeling of disinterest.

6 Some people laugh when they are nervous or feel confronted. Inappropriate laughing can cause even more friction in a difficult situation. Work on developing a calm facial expression that reflects the fact that you really do care about what's happening.

7 Never overlook the importance of a simple smile or wave of recognition. You may be on the phone ordering a case of glue, but you can still give a wave to acknowledge a parent who is leaving the building or a staff member who has just arrived.

8 Silence is appropriate in many conversations. Nodding your head and communicating with "Ah-ha" or "Mmm" encourages the other person to complete his or her thoughts. Allowing for a pause or silence helps people feel they can express themselves without fear of interruption.

9 Do you often stand with your arms folded in front of you? This posture can give others the impression of indifference or inaccessibility.

10 It takes 30 seconds to make a first impression. If parents see you or other employees with dour expressions or slouched in chairs, their image of your center is greatly influenced by your nonverbal communication.

Staff Problem Solving

1 When there is a problem, ask each staff member to summarize it in writing, in 25 words or less. This condenses the situation and avoids long-winded explanations that place blame and add unnecessary details.

2 In group discussions, set a rule that interruptions are not permitted. People need to know they can finish their thoughts before someone else expresses an opposing opinion. If someone tries to interrupt you, respond, "I'll be glad to listen to you as soon as I finish the point I want to make."

3 Rephrase a staff member's complaint to make sure you understand the point. "What I think you meant is that you want ideas on how to stop Megan from coming back from her break 10 minutes late."

4 When trying to promote staff problem solving, avoid asking closed questions such as, "Did the parents arrive late?" Instead, ask open-ended questions such as, "What do you think we should do about parents who pick up their children late?" Asking closed questions promotes one- or two-word answers that are seldom useful in solving problems. Effective problem solving requires going beyond yes or no questions to find out what is really happening.

5 Complaining employees may simply need a chance to vent a frustration. Often, careful listening reveals that the complaint is the manifestation of a deeper problem. If a staff member is going through a divorce or is caring for an aging parent, he or she may express frustration by complaining about something completely unrelated, such as the lack of purple paint. Knowing what's behind the complaint helps you deal with the real issue.

6 When an employee complains to you, never express agreement with the situation with a comment like, "I know what you mean. She bothers me also." You may appear to be taking sides. Remain neutral until you know all the facts.

7 When a person complains to you on a regular basis, ask him or her to write the problem in memo form and include various solutions. Many people won't make the effort to do that, or they will develop a solution of their own in the process.

8 When a complaining employee has unrealistic expectations, provide some facts. A balance sheet showing the cost of a new playground relative to current annual income and expenses would be concrete proof that the idea is impractical at this time. The employee will appreciate the fact that you took the time to show him or her facts rather than simply saying, "It's too expensive."

9 When an employee complains chronically about a particular solution, respond with this question, "What would you do if you were the director of this center?" The question forces the employee to look at the problem from a different perspective. Conversely, the employee may have a great idea you never thought about.

10 Employees frequently complain that they have too many responsibilities and duties. Ask them for ways to streamline communication procedures. Is too much paperwork involved? Can you eliminate unnecessary activity? What stands in the way of allowing your employees to serve the children in their care? You may find that the complaints are valid and the problems can be corrected by using checklists or standardized forms, or by making schedule changes.

Use Totline® Resources

When you need ideas for helping young children learn and grow, turn to Totline books and resources. Totline Publications is committed to providing quality

resources for directors, teachers,

daycare providers, parents, and others who work with children ages 2 to 8. The useful ideas presented in Totline Books are easy to implement; and require only common, inexpensive materials. Our hands-on, around-the-curriculum activities make learning fun for everyone.